ENCOMIUM OF HELEN

GORGIAS
ENCOMIUM OF HELEN

EDITED WITH INTRODUCTION,
NOTES AND TRANSLATION
BY D.M. MacDOWELL
PROFESSOR OF GREEK IN
THE UNIVERSITY OF GLASGOW

PUBLISHED BY BRISTOL CLASSICAL PRESS
GENERAL EDITOR: JOHN H. BETTS

This impression 2005
First published in 1982 by
Bristol Classical Press
an imprint of
Gerald Duckworth & Co. Ltd.
90-93 Cowcross Street, London EC1M 6BF
Tel: 020 7490 7300
Fax: 020 7490 0080
inquiries@duckworth-publishers.co.uk
www.ducknet.co.uk

A catalogue record for this book is available
from the British Library

ISBN 0 86292 053 1

Cover illustration: Woman making offering of ointment or jewellery
from a mid-fifth century *stele*, Staatlichemuseum, Berlin

Contents

Preface

Students of Greek prose literature are regularly told that Gorgias is a figure of great importance in its development, but his work is not easily accessible to them unless they are prepared to tackle the formidable volumes of Diels-Kranz. In 1972 therefore I prepared this little edition to assist undergraduates to read one short but complete work of Gorgias, and the Honours Class of Greek in Glasgow has used it for ten years in a samizdat form. Now the kindness of Mr John Betts in agreeing to produce it as a Bristol Classical Press edition has given me an occasion to revise it, including references to work published recently by several scholars. Its chief purpose is still to help readers approaching Gorgias for the first time, rather than to make a substantial contribution to scholarship. Nevertheless, although no *apparatus criticus* is included, some of the most serious textual difficulties are noted in the commentary, and cognoscenti will find several places where I have made a new suggestion about the text or its interpretation.

D.M.M.
University of Glasgow
March 1982

Select Bibliography

For the Greek text of all surviving works and fragments of Gorgias, with *apparatus criticus*, see *Die Fragmente der Vorsokratiker*, edited by H. Diels and W. Kranz (sixth edition 1952) vol. 2 no. 82. There is an English translation by G. Kennedy in *The Older Sophists*, edited by R.K. Sprague (1972).

For a full bibliography of modern work on Gorgias up to 1975, see *Sophistik*, edited by C.J. Classen (*Wege der Forschung* 187, 1976) 683-9.

Bona, G., 'Λόγος e ἀλήθεια nell'*Encomio di Elena* di Gorgia', *Rivista di Filologia* 102 (1974) 5-33.

Calogero, G., 'Gorgias and the Socratic principle *nemo sua sponte peccat*', *Journal of Hellenic Studies* 77 (1957) 12-17.

Denniston, J.D., *Greek Prose Style* (1952) ch. 1.

Dodds, E.R., *Plato: Gorgias* (1959) 6-10.

Donadi, F., 'Esplorazioni alla tradizione manoscritta dell'*Encomio di Elena* gorgiano', *Bollettino dell'Istituto di Filologia Greca, Padova* 2 (1975) 170-84, 3 (1976) 225-50.

———— 'Gorgia, *Elena* 16', *Bollettino dell'Istituto di Filologia Greca, Padova* 4 (1977-8) 48-77.

Finley, J.H., 'The origins of Thucydides' style', *Harvard Studies in Classical Philology* 50 (1939) 35-84, reprinted in his *Three Essays on Thucydides* (1967).

Guthrie, W.K.C., *A History of Greek Philosophy* vol. 3 (1969) part 1, reprinted in paperback as *The Sophists*.

Harrison, E.L., 'Was Gorgias a sophist?', *Phoenix* 18 (1964) 183-92.

Immisch, O., *Gorgiae Helena* (1927).

Kennedy, G., *The Art of Persuasion in Greece* (1963).

Kerferd, G.B., *The Sophistic Movement* (1981).

MacDowell, D.M., 'Gorgias, Alkidamas, and the Cripps and Palatine manuscripts', *Classical Quarterly* n.s. 11 (1961) 113-24.

Newiger, H.-J., *Untersuchungen zu Gorgias' Schrift Über das Nichtseiende* (1973).

Robinson, J.M., 'On Gorgias', in *Exegesis and Argument, studies presented to G. Vlastos, Phronesis* supp. vol. 1 (1973) 49-60.

Romilly, J. de, *Magic and Rhetoric in Ancient Greece* (1975).

——— 'Gorgias et le pouvoir de la poésie', *Journal of Hellenic Studies* 93 (1973) 155-62.

Rosenmeyer, T.G., 'Gorgias, Aeschylus, and *apate*', *American Journal of Philology* 76 (1955) 225-60.

Segal, C.P., 'Gorgias and the psychology of the *logos*', *Harvard Studies in Classical Philology* 66 (1962) 99-155.

Verdenius, W.J., 'Gorgias' doctrine of deception', in *The Sophists and their Legacy*, edited by G.B. Kerferd, *Hermes* Einzelschriften 44 (1981) 116-28.

Introduction

The Life and Works of Gorgias

Gorgias, son of Kharmantides, was born at Leontinoi in Sicily. The date of his birth is not known, but no doubt it was between 490 and 460 BC. He is said to have been a disciple of the philosopher-scientist Empedokles (Diogenes Laertios 8.58, *Souda* γ 388, cf. Plato *Menon* 76c), and is mentioned by Isokrates (10.3, 15.268) alongside other philosophers of Sicily and south Italy in the mid-fifth century, such as Parmenides, Zenon, and Melissos. The first datable event in his life is that he wrote his book *On What is Not, or On Nature* in the eighty-fourth Olympiad, which was in 444-1 (Olympiodoros *Commentary on Plato's Gorgias* prooemium 9).

He became known as an orator, and in 427, when Leontinoi was attacked by Syracuse, the Leontines appointed him leader of the envoys whom they sent to their ally Athens to ask for military help. His oratory amazed the Athenians, who evidently had heard nothing like it before. Help was sent, and Gorgias returned to Leontinoi amid general admiration (Diodoros 12.53; cf. Thucydides 3.86, Plato *Hippias the greater* 282b, Timaios in Dionysios of Halikarnassos *Lysias* 3 = Jacoby *Fragmente der greichischen Historiker* 566 F 137).

After that, as far as we know, he spent the rest of his life giving instruction and displays of oratory. He had no wife or children, and did not settle permanently in any one city, but travelled around living on fees which he charged for his teaching. In particular, he spent some time teaching at Larisa in Thessaly (Isokrates 15.155-6, Plato *Menon* 70b, Aristotle *Politics* 1275b 26-30). Plato's *Gorgias*, in which he appears as a leading character, shows that he became a familiar figure in Athens. He was still alive when that work was written, and remarked sarcastically that Plato was a good satirist: ὡς καλῶς οἶδε Πλάτων ἰαμβίζειν (Athenaios 505d). He was honoured by Iason, the ruler of Pherai in Thessaly, which indicates that he lived until 380 or later, and he was over a hundred years old when he died: different authorities give different ages, ranging from 105 to 109 (Pausanias 6.17.9, Philostratos *Lives of Sophists* 1.9, *Souda* γ 388). When someone asked him how he reached such a great age in good health, he replied 'Because I have never done anything for pleasure' (Athenaios 548d).

9

Gorgias is one of the best examples of the men called 'sophists', who in the second half of the fifth century made a profession of teaching intellectual subjects to anyone willing to pay for it. The subject which he taught was rhetoric. He did not claim, as some of his contemporaries did, to teach 'virtue', ἀρετή, but thought that his function was simply to make men clever at speaking (Plato *Menon* 95c). For the function of rhetoric is to persuade, and you can control all arts and skills if you can persuade other people to exercise them or not to exercise them as you wish; therefore rhetoric, in Gorgias' view, is the supreme art (Plato *Philebos* 58a, *Gorgias* 453a).

His teaching probably consisted mainly of demonstration and display; he would deliver a speech, and his pupils would listen and observe how it was done. He also gave them model speeches in writing to be learned by heart (Aristotle *Sophistical Refutations* 183b 37), and, as we see from Plato's *Gorgias*, he offered to give an answer to any question asked. Aristotle tells us that he said that one should demolish one's opponents' seriousness by humour, and their humour by seriousness (*Rhetoric* 1419b 4-5), which shows that he gave theoretical advice in addition to practical demonstration; and some such advice was in writing – possibly a kind of handbook for his pupils (Dionysios of Halikarnassos *Composition* 12). But there is no evidence that he ever heard or criticised his pupils' speeches.

The only complete works of Gorgias which survive are his short *Encomium of Helen* and the slightly longer *Defence of Palamedes*. Each of these is an ingenious defence of a mythical person traditionally regarded as bad or immoral. Presumably their purpose is to show how skilful argument can make even the worst case seem good; and Gorgias will have delivered them orally or distributed them in writing to his pupils or to the general public, in order to show his own skill as a rhetorician and suggest types of argument which prospective orators could use for weak cases.

We have one paragraph in which Gorgias praises Athenians who have been killed in war; this very likely belongs to the *Funeral Speech* (ἐπιτάφιος) from which we have one or two other short quotations, including the striking reference to vultures as ζῶντας τάφους, 'living tombs' (fragment 5a). One might suppose that this was the speech delivered in some year at the annual public funeral of Athenians killed in war, like the speech of Perikles reported by Thucydides in Book 2. On the other hand, it seems unlikely that the privilege of making the speech on such an important Athenian occasion would have been given to someone who was not an Athenian citizen. Perhaps the speech was composed by Gorgias for an Athenian to deliver; or perhaps it was just a demonstration model of what such a speech should be like.

There was also an *Olympic Speech*, delivered to the Greeks assembled for the festival at Olympia, on the subject of Greek unity, from which a few fragments survive; a *Pythian Speech*, delivered at the festival at Delphi, from which nothing survives; and an *Encomium to the Eleians*, beginning 'Elis is a lucky city' (fragments 7-10). Each of these sounds like a public speech intended to show off Gorgias' rhetorical skill to a wide audience – and so, perhaps, to attract pupils.

The only other written work of Gorgias which is known is his treatise *On What Is Not, or On Nature* (Περὶ τοῦ μὴ ὄντος, ἢ Περὶ φύσεως). Though this work does not survive, fairly detailed accounts of it are given by [Aristotle] *Melissos, Xenophanes and Gorgias* 979a 11 – 980b 21 and Sextos Empeirikos *Against Mathematicians* 7.65-87. It offered proofs of three propositions: (a) nothing is; (b) even if it is, it is incomprehensible to man; (c) even if it is comprehensible, it is incommunicable to the next man. The purpose and significance of this work have been much discussed in modern times. Was it a serious contribution to philosophy, or merely a display of skill at argument? Some scholars (for example, E.R. Dodds, *Plato: Gorgias* 7-8) have regarded it as just a piece of fun, and there is much to be said in favour of that view. It certainly appears at first sight to be ludicrous to argue at length that what does not exist does not exist, and that what exists does not exist, and then (as if that were not enough) that what exists and what does not exist do not both exist; it seems like a comic parody of Parmenides and others who wrote books entitled *On Nature, or On What Is*. An English reader presented with a play entitled *Thirteenth Night, or What You Won't* would be in no doubt that a joke was intended; perhaps the reaction of a Greek to a book entitled *On What Isn't* was similar. Yet parody can have a serious purpose too, and some scholars (for example, W.K.C. Guthrie, *History of Greek Philosophy* 3.192-200) hold that Gorgias wished to refute the philosophical views of Parmenides by reducing them to absurdity. That would still imply that Gorgias did not himself believe his own conclusions to be literally true, and it is indeed hard to think that Gorgias seriously believed that nothing exists. But recently a new dimension has been given to the discussion by reinterpretation of the verb 'to be', εἶναι, in a sense which is more predicative than existential. Perhaps Gorgias did not mean to argue that nothing exists, but rather that nothing is identical with any other thing or quality; if so, that strengthens considerably the claim that he may be regarded as a serious philosopher. The question cannot be discussed in detail here. For a full discussion see H.-J. Newiger, *Untersuchungen zu Gorgias' Schrift Über das Nichtseiende* (1973); for a short discussion in English, interpreting the work seriously and attempting to place Gorgias in the development of philosophy, see G.B. Kerferd *The Sophistic Movement* 93-100.

Even if the treatise *On What Is Not, or On Nature* is accepted as showing that Gorgias was a philosopher, it is important to bear in mind that it is an early work, dated to the years 444-1 (Olympiodoros, *Commentary on Plato's Gorgias*

11

prooemium 9). There is no evidence that he maintained an interest in philosophy, as distinct from rhetoric, later in his life – unless we think we can find such evidence in his *Encomium of Helen*.

The Encomium of Helen

The subject of Gorgias' encomium is the most notorious woman in Greek mythology: Helen, who deserted her husband Menelaos, king of Sparta, to elope with Paris (also called Alexander), a prince of Troy. Discussion of the guilt or innocence of Helen is probably as old as the myth itself; we can trace it back to Homer (*Iliad* 3.164). Euripides gives us a formal debate on the question between Helen and Hecuba in *Trojan Women* 914-1032, and in a later play, *Helen*, he follows an alternative version of the myth which exculpates Helen by telling that it was not herself but only a phantom of her that went to Troy. Attempts have been made to date Gorgias' work in relation to those plays; but was Euripides answering Gorgias or Gorgias answering Euripides? Probably neither. There is no resemblance in details, and no strong reason to link Gorgias' discussion of Helen with anyone else's.

He begins with a short introductory passage in which he says that his purpose is to show that it is wrong to blame Helen. He gives a brief account of her birth and marriage, and then comes to the question: why did Helen go to Troy? He says that four causes are possible: Chance and the gods; force; persuasive speech; love. He discusses each of the four in turn (the gods in 6, force in 7, speech in 8-14, love in 15-19), and argues that each is a mighty power, so that Helen should not be blamed for submitting to it. He then concludes in a couple of sentences that he has done what he set out to do. What he does is not in fact to praise Helen, but to defend her conduct against criticism; *Defence of Helen* would really have been a more appropriate title.

Up to a point the argument is convincing. It is possible to agree that Helen, if she did elope with Paris, must have been subject to at least one of the four influences listed. (One may disbelieve in one or two of them; nor are they mutually exclusive; but neither of these facts affects the validity of Gorgias' argument.) And if one believes that her action was caused either by the gods or by force, one may well accept that she should not be blamed for it.

But the most important and interesting passage is the one about λόγος (8-14, one third of the whole work). Speech, says Gorgias in his best known sentence, is a powerful ruler (λόγος δυνάστης μέγας ἐστίν); it can arouse or subdue fear, sorrow, joy, and pity. It compels the mind; so if Helen was persuaded by speech to do as she did, she acted under compulsion.

What does he mean by λόγος, and how does he think it works? The word λόγος is a difficult one; Liddell and Scott (revised by Jones) devote more space to it in their lexicon than to any other word, and their long article deserves careful study. But essentially Gorgias uses it to mean any kind of speech or speaking (rather than calculation or other processes of thought). Thus it may be 'a speech' in formal circumstances, such as a legal trial, but it may equally be any other use of words, in scientific or philosophical discussion (13), poetry (9), or magical incantations (10). A λόγος may be in writing (cf. 13 γραφείς), but in the time of Gorgias it was probably always assumed that written words would be read out orally. Thus the *Encomium of Helen* itself is a λόγος (3); alternatively, it is a number of λόγοι, for a λόγος may be just one passage or part of speech (cf. 15 τῷ τετάρτῳ λόγῳ). There is one place where Gorgias does use the word to mean 'relation' (14 τὸν αὐτὸν λόγον ἔχει), though even there he may be thinking of spoken words, and we could translate 'can be spoken of in the same way'. For 'reasoning' he uses not λόγος but another word, etymologically connected, λογισμός (2).

Speech can be either true or false. That may appear too obvious to need saying; but in the present context it is necessary to say it, because some modern scholars have declared that in Gorgias' view speech is never true but always involves deception, ἀπάτη. Thus most recently W.J. Verdenius has elevated this into a philosophical doctrine, 'Gorgias' doctrine of deception' (in *The Sophists and their Legacy*, ed. G.B. Kerferd). There seem to be three reasons for attributing such a view to Gorgias:

1. Gorgias argues that Helen may have been deceived by speech (8 ἀπατήσας), and supports his argument by giving other examples of deceptive speech. But obviously that is because truthful speech is not relevant to his argument here; giving examples of deceptive speech does not amount to saying that no speech is true. (Verdenius, op. cit. 116, distorts the evidence by mistranslation; e.g. 11 ὅσοι, meaning 'how many...!' is converted by him into '*all* his arguments are *equally* "fictitious and false"' [my italics].)

2. Plutarch, in a comment on tragedy (*Ethika* 348c = Diels-Kranz 82 B 23), tells us that Gorgias called tragedy a deception in which 'he who deceives is honester than he who does not deceive, and he who is deceived is wiser than he who is not deceived. He who deceives is honester because he has done what he undertook to do; he who is deceived is wiser, because what is not imperceptive is easily captivated by pleasure of speech.' This antithetical parodox is exactly in the manner of Gorgias, and is surely a genuine fragment of some work of his. But it is not a comment on speech in general, but on theatrical performance, in which an actor impersonates a character; the actor 'deceives' by pretending to be Oedipus or Electra, which is what he is engaged to do, and the intelligent spectator 'is deceived' when he shares in the illusion by a willing suspension of disbelief. So this comment on drama has no relevance to other kinds of speech.

13

3. In his work *On What Is Not* Gorgias argued that nothing is, nothing is knowable, and nothing is communicable. It follows from this that speech cannot communicate the truth.

Of these three reasons, only the third really provides any basis for supposing that Gorgias believed that speech is invariably deceptive. Here we meet again the problem, already mentioned, how far Gorgias meant his work *On What Is Not* to be taken seriously and literally. However, our concern here is with the *Encomium of Helen*; and in the *Encomium* it is quite certain that speech can be true. In the very first sentence Gorgias declares that the merit of λόγος (that is, the thing which makes a speech a good speech) is truth, and he goes on to say that the purpose of this particular speech is to show what is true (2 δεῖξαι τἀληθές) and to put a stop to the ignorance of opinion (21 καταλῦσαι...δόξης ἀμαθίαν). This has been pointed out well by G. Bona (*Riv. Fil.* 102 [1974] 5-33). Bona then tries to reconcile this with the argument of *On What Is Not* by suggesting that Gorgias believes only that matters of experience and contingent fact cannot be expressed by speech, but it is quite possible to make a true statement of logic or reasoning; indeed *On What Is Not* must itself have consisted of statements which Gorgias believed to be true on logical grounds, and so does much of the *Encomium of Helen*, in which he argues not that Helen went to Troy for a particular reason in fact but that it is logically wrong to blame her whatever her reason may have been. However, it is doubtful whether Gorgias' consistency should be defended by this distinction between statements of reason and statements of fact. In 11 Gorgias says 'How many men have persuaded and do persuade how many, on how many subjects, by fabricating false speech! For if everyone, on every subject, possessed memory of the past and <understanding> of the present and foreknowledge of the future, speech would not be equally <powerful>; but as it is, neither remembering a past event nor investigating a present one nor prophesying a future one is easy, so that on most subjects most men make belief their mind's adviser. But belief, being slippery and unreliable, brings slippery and unreliable success to those who employ it'. This certainly implies that people sometimes do have knowledge of contingent facts; to attain such knowledge is not impossible but merely difficult, and only when they lack knowledge (which is very often, but still not always) do they have to resort to opinion or belief, δόξα (which brings unreliable success; that is, it is sometimes right and sometimes wrong). It probably, though less clearly, implies also that what they say, or what others say to them, may be either in accordance or in conflict with the facts; that is, that speech may be either true or false. It seems best to conclude, therefore, that in this matter the *Encomium of Helen* does not say the same thing as *On What Is Not*. Whether that is because Gorgias changed his mind (the two works may have been written many years apart) or because he never did believe the argument of *On What Is*

14

Not is a question which may be left open here.

But the thing which most interests Gorgias about speech, in the *Encomium of Helen*, is not so much its use to state facts, but its use to arouse emotions and influence behaviour. It can produce fear, sorrow, joy or pity (8). This function of speech has no necessary connection with truth or falsehood; if you tell a man that he is about to be killed, his feeling of alarm will be exactly the same whether your words are true or false, as long as he believes them. Getting him to believe them is persuasion, πειθώ. Persuasion is something which may be added to speech (cf. 13 ἡ πειθὼ προσιοῦσα τῷ λόγῳ) to make it effective; Gorgias does not define it more exactly, but presumably it is, or at least includes, the art of rhetoric. Speech combined with persuasion acts upon the mind of the hearer, and stamps or moulds it in the desired form (13 τὴν ψυχὴν ἐτυπώσατο ὅπως ἐβούλετο). It affects the mind in much the same way as drugs affect the body. Some drugs benefit the body and others harm it; likewise speech may do either harm or good to the mind, instilling sorrow or pleasure, fear or courage (14). Gorgias does not say that an emotion produced by true speech is beneficial and an emotion produced by false speech is harmful, and so it remains obscure whether he thinks it possible to do good to a person by telling him a lie; but in the case of Helen, at least, his suggestion is that false speech had a harmful effect.

No sharp distinction is made between getting someone to believe something and getting him to do something. The verb πείθομαι means both 'believe' and 'obey'; and this verbal ambiguity (which is not confined to Gorgias) implies that belief and action normally go together. In modern times we are familiar with the notion that one may, while convinced that one ought to do a certain thing, actually do something different. Among the Greeks that notion, though not unknown, was less common; the principle 'no one does wrong intentionally', generally associated with Sokrates, is also implicit in Gorgias (as C. Calogero has shown in *JHS* 77 [1957] 12-17). Indeed, for the purpose of his defence of Helen, Gorgias presents the whole process as one of strict cause and effect: not only does action follow inevitably from belief, but belief follows inevitably from persuasive speech. Just as the body cannot choose but obey a powerful drug, so the mind cannot choose but obey a powerful speech. If a speaker has mastered the art of rhetoric, he can compel other people to do anything he wishes; not only is that implied by the argument in the *Encomium of Helen* (12), but Plato also attributes that view to Gorgias in his *Gorgias* (e.g. 452e). If we accept Gorgias' claim that speech is as powerful as that, it follows logically that we must blame the persuader, not the persuaded person, for any evil result: ὁ πείσας ὡς ἀναγκάσας ἀδικεῖ, 'the persuader, because he compelled, is guilty' (12).

Analogous to Gorgias' treatment of λόγος is his treatment of love, ἔρως, the fourth possible cause of Helen's departure to Troy. Whereas speech reaches the mind by way of hearing, sexual desire operates through sight. This impression involves mental pictures (17 εἰκόνας...ἐν τῷ φρονήματι), and also affects a person's behaviour (15 ἡ ψυχὴ κἂν τοῖς τρόποις τυποῦται). Just as Gorgias earlier gave examples of different kinds of powerful speech, so he also gives examples of different kinds of powerful sight: the sight of an enemy army causes alarm and makes men run away even before they are in danger (16); paintings and sculpture arouse pleasure, giving the eyes 'a pleasant disease' (18). The conclusion is that sexual desire, like speech, exercises compulsion (19 ἔρωτος ἀνάγκαις).

The suggestion that love is a force so strong that no one can resist it is not a new one. Sophokles has a choral ode about invincible ἔρως (Antigone 781-800; cf. Women of Trakhis 441-8 and the remark attributed to Sophokles in Plato Republic 329c). Sometimes Ἔρως is regarded as a god, and then it can be argued that naturally a human being cannot be expected to be stronger than a divine one (Aristophanes Clouds 1082, Euripides Helen 948-50). Alternatively it may be regarded as a kind of disease (Sophokles Women of Trakhis 445, Euripides Hippolytos 394, etc.). But those are passages of poetic imagery and exaggeration. In ordinary life perhaps few people regard love as a force so compelling that it justifies any and every kind of misconduct. Gorgias fails to allow for different degrees of misconduct and different degrees of love.

Many readers, then, are likely to consider that Gorgias overstates his case, and that speech and love are not as irresistible as he suggests. Does he even believe it himself? In the very last word he reveals that his encomium of Helen is a game, παίγνιον. Some serious scholars, evidently horrified at the notion that a rhetorical text might be fun, either ignore this word or claim that Gorgias does not really mean it. But there is no reason to reject it. Thrasymakhos too wrote παίγνια (Souda ϑ 462), and it may well have been a regular activity of rhetoricians. One may compare a modern legal moot. Plainly Gorgias enjoys showing off his rhetorical skill in defending conduct which is really indefensible. In a real trial much depends on the speech for the defence, perhaps even life or death; but Helen is a mythical personage, and neither Gorgias nor anyone else is really worried about her innocence.

Nevertheless, all that we know of Gorgias, including the very fact that it amused him to construct a defence of the indefensible, confirms that he genuinely believed speech to be a most effective instrument for influencing people's minds and actions. He devoted most of his life to rhetoric. Probably no one before him had ever given so much attention to it, and so his remarks about its nature have a special interest. Although I doubt whether the Encomium of Helen ought to be called a work of philosophy, surely the comments on speech give us his real opinion and understanding of that subject. The reason why he is a significant figure in the history of literature and thought is that he drew attention to the power of words.

Prose Style

τῷ ξενίζοντι τῆς λέξεως ἐξέπληξε τοὺς ᾿Αθηναίους, 'he astounded the Athenians by the strangeness of his speech', says Diodoros (12.53.3). What was this strangeness of utterance which caused amazement in 427 BC? Hardly just a foreign accent; the Athenians had heard Sicilians before. There must, rather, have been features of Gorgias' choice and arrangement of words which were new to Athens. But our difficulty, as we read the *Encomium of Helen* and the other surviving pieces of his work, is in telling which of the features which we observe in them were new to Athens in 427 and which were not. For one thing, we have very little Attic prose of an earlier date to compare them with. For another, we do not know whether the surviving texts of Gorgias accurately represent his style as it was at that date. The *Encomium of Helen* and the *Defence of Palamedes* are written entirely in Attic Greek, not in the Sicilian dialect which one might have expected Gorgias to use. That suggests that they were not written at the time of his first visit to Athens, but long afterwards, when he had adopted Attic as being the best dialect for literary composition. Yet even this is uncertain, for we cannot rule out the possibility that Gorgias actually did write these works in his native dialect and they were Atticised by some later editor.

However, we can still make an attempt to identify in the surviving texts the stylistic feature or features likely to have impressed the Athenians. Three possibilities seem worth considering, though perhaps only the third deserves acceptance.

1. Aristotle remarks that Gorgias' λέξις is poetic (*Rhetoric* 1404a 26). From Aristotle's use of the term λέξις elsewhere it may be taken as certain that he means 'choice of words', but he gives no detailed evidence for his remark, and it is not easy to believe that it has much value. It is true that there are two or three words in the *Encomium of Helen* which seldom or never occur in classical Attic prose (e.g. 1 μῶμον, 9 φιλοπενθής). But such words are not really very numerous; and in any case a comparison with fourth-century Attic prose may be misleading. We do not have adequate evidence that the differences between poetic and prose vocabulary which existed in the fourth century had already emerged in the fifth. It is possible that Gorgias' vocabulary is simply the ordinary vocabulary of his day, used in poetry and prose alike, and that it merely seemed poetic to Aristotle and his contemporaries because by their time greater differences between poetic and prose vocabulary had developed.

2. Gorgias' arrangement of topics is remarkably orderly and well-

signposted. He announces what he is going to say; he says it; he points out that he has now completed it. '(6) Either it was because of the wishes of Chance and the purposes of the gods and the decrees of Necessity that she did what she did, or because she was seized by force, or persuaded by speeches, or <captivated by love>. Now, if it was because of the first... (7) But if she was seized by force... (8) But if it was love that brought all this about... (20)... Whether she did what she did because she was enamoured by sight or persuaded by speech or seized by force or compelled by divine necessity, in every case she escapes the accusation. (21) I have removed by my speech a woman's infamy, I have kept to the purpose which I set myself at the start of my speech...' Yet this may have been a common feature of early prose. Herodotus too sometimes announces what he is going to say, and later points out that he has said it; and his work was probably known to Athenians before 427. So it does not seem likely that orderliness of arrangement was the feature of Gorgias which bowled the Athenians over.

3. There remains the feature of Gorgias' style which strikes most readers as being the most prominent of all: his use of antithesis and pairs of parallel expressions. In sentence after sentence, individual words and longer phrases are set side by side to produce symmetry in grammar and sound. Gorgias did not, of course, invent antithesis; μέν / δέ and τε / καί existed long before his time, and it is not hard to find pairs of parallel phrases or sentences in Attic tragedy and other poetry. (A good account of this, showing that the style of Gorgias was not quite as revolutionary as has sometimes been thought, and should not be assumed to have had a decisive influence on the styles of Antiphon and Thucydides, is given by J.H. Finley *Three Essays on Thucydides* 55-88.) But in Gorgias anthitheses are more frequent, more compact, and more precisely balanced. Sometimes two phrases are so exactly equalized that even their scansion is identical, e.g. 3 ὁ μὲν ἀνδρῶν κράτιστος, ὁ δὲ πάντων τύραννος. Sometimes two words rhyme or in some other way resemble each other in sound, e.g. 2 ὁμόφωνος καὶ ὁμόψυχος, 4 λαβοῦσα καὶ οὐ λαθοῦσα. Sometimes the same word is used twice with different inflections (the figure of speech called polyptoton or etymological figure), e.g. 4 ἑνὶ δὲ σώματι πολλὰ σώματα, and this may even be done with two different words arranged chiastically, e.g. 7 ὁ μὲν ἐπιχειρήσας βάρβαρος βάρβαρον ἐπιχείρημα. Altogether antithesis and parallelism are used far more often by Gorgias than by any other Greek author, as far as our knowledge goes; and so it seems quite likely that (as Diodoros 12.53.4 suggests) this was what struck the Athenians as novel in 427.

But if so, one may still wonder whether the Athenians were right to admire Gorgias on that account. At least one of the greatest modern connoisseurs of Greek prose style, J.D. Denniston, was sure that they were not. He accused Gorgias of exaggerating balance and antithesis to the point of absurdity:

'starting with the initial advantage of having nothing in particular to say, he was able to concentrate all his energies upon saying it' (*Greek Prose Style* 10-12). Those who believe that the best style is that which arises naturally out of the subject matter will share Denniston's views. It is certainly true that Gorgias' style is something artificially imposed on his material. Matter which does not contain any inherent contrast is split in half or duplicated for the sole purpose of producing a pair. Even in a short phrase like φόβον παῦσαι καὶ λύπην ἀφελεῖν (8) the second infinitive expresses no meaning not already expressed by the first, and has been added simply for the sake of having two infinitives alongside the two nouns. Often things are made to sound more alike than they really are; for example, one trick is to use a pair of genitives, of which one is subjective and the other objective, so that they sound similar although their syntactical function is actually different, as in ψυχῆς ἀγρεύμασιν, οὐ γνώμης βουλεύμασι (19; cf. the note on 2 τῶν συμφορῶν μνήμη). Yet a less austere view than Denniston's remains possible. Stylistic devices can sometimes stimulate or amuse even when the subject matter does not imperatively demand them. Ornamentation may be either attractive or unattractive, but it is not immoral; and whether he finds Gorgias' type of ornamentation attractive or irritating is a question which each reader may decide for himself.

ΓΟΡΓΙΟΥ ΕΛΕΝΗΣ ΕΓΚΩΜΙΟΝ

Κόσμος πόλει μὲν εὐανδρία, σώματι δὲ κάλλος, ψυχῇ δὲ σοφία, πράγματι δὲ ἀρετή, λόγῳ δὲ ἀλήθεια· τὰ δὲ ἐναντία τούτων ἀκοσμία. ἄνδρα δὲ καὶ γυναῖκα καὶ λόγον καὶ ἔργον καὶ πόλιν καὶ πρᾶγμα χρὴ τὸ μὲν ἄξιον ἐπαίνου ἐπαίνῳ τιμᾶν, τῷ δὲ ἀναξίῳ μῶμον ἐπιθεῖναι· ἴση γὰρ ἁμαρτία καὶ ἀμαθία μέμφεσθαί τε τὰ ἐπαινετὰ

2 καὶ ἐπαινεῖν τὰ μωμητά. τοῦ δ᾽ αὐτοῦ ἀνδρὸς λέξαι τε τὸ δέον ὀρθῶς καὶ ἐλέγξαι τοὺς μεμφομένους Ἑλένην, γυναῖκα περὶ ἧς ὁμόφωνος καὶ ὁμόψυχος γέγονεν ἥ τε τῶν ποιητῶν ἀκουσάντων πίστις ἥ τε τοῦ ὀνόματος φήμη, ὃ τῶν συμφορῶν μνήμη γέγονεν. ἐγὼ δὲ βούλομαι λογισμόν τινα τῷ λόγῳ δοὺς τὴν μὲν κακῶς ἀκούουσαν παῦσαι τῆς αἰτίας, τοὺς δὲ μεμφομένους ψευδομένους ἐπιδεῖξαι, καὶ δεῖξαί τε τἀληθὲς καὶ παῦσαι τῆς ἀμαθίας.

3 Ὅτι μὲν οὖν φύσει καὶ γένει τὰ πρῶτα τῶν πρώτων ἀνδρῶν καὶ γυναικῶν ἡ γυνὴ περὶ ἧς ὅδε ὁ λόγος, οὐκ ἄδηλον οὐδὲ ὀλίγοις. δῆλον γὰρ ὡς μητρὸς μὲν Λήδας, πατρὸς δὲ τοῦ μὲν γενομένου θεοῦ, λεγομένου δὲ θνητοῦ, Τυνδάρεω καὶ Διός, ὧν ὁ μὲν διὰ τὸ εἶναι ἔδοξεν, ὁ δὲ διὰ τὸ φάναι ἐλέχθη, καὶ ἦν ὁ μὲν

4 ἀνδρῶν κράτιστος, ὁ δὲ πάντων τύραννος. ἐκ τοιούτων δὲ γενομένη ἔσχε τὸ ἰσόθεον κάλλος, ὃ λαβοῦσα καὶ οὐ λαθοῦσα ἔσχε. πλείστας δὲ πλείστοις ἐπιθυμίας ἔρωτος ἐνηργάσατο· ἑνὶ δὲ σώματι πολλὰ σώματα συνήγαγεν ἀνδρῶν ἐπὶ μεγάλοις μέγα φρονούντων ὧν οἱ μὲν πλούτου μεγέθη, οἱ δὲ εὐγενείας παλαιᾶς εὐδοξίαν, οἱ δὲ ἀλκῆς ἰδίας εὐεξίαν, οἱ δὲ σοφίας ἐπικτήτου δύναμιν ἔσχον· καὶ ἧκον ἅπαντες ὑπ ἔρωτός τε φιλονίκου φιλοτιμίας τε ἀνικήτου.

5 ὅστις μὲν οὖν καὶ δι᾽ ὅ τι καὶ ὅπως ἀπέπλησε τὸν ἔρωτα τὴν Ἑλένην λαβών, οὐ λέξω· τὸ γὰρ τοῖς εἰδόσιν ἃ ἴσασι λέγειν πίστιν μὲν ἔχει, τέρψιν δὲ οὐ φέρει. τὸν χρόνον δὲ τῷ λόγῳ τὸν τότε νῦν ὑπερβὰς ἐπὶ τὴν ἀρχὴν τοῦ μέλλοντος λόγου προβήσομαι, καὶ προθήσομαι τὰς αἰτίας, δι᾽ ἃς εἰκὸς ἦν γενέσθαι τὸν τῆς Ἑλένης εἰς τὴν Τροίαν στόλον.

GORGIAS' ENCOMIUM OF HELEN

The grace of a city is excellence of its men, of a body beauty, of a mind wisdom, of an action virtue, of a speech truth; the opposites of these are a disgrace. A man, a woman, a speech, a deed, a city, and an action, if deserving praise, one should honour with praise, but to the undeserving one should attach blame. For it is an equal error and ignorance to blame the praiseworthy and to praise the blameworthy. The man who says rightly what ought to be said should also refute 2 those who blame Helen, a woman about whom both the belief of those who have listened to poets and the message of her name, which has become a reminder of the calamities, have been in unison and unanimity. I wish, by adding some reasoning to my speech, to free the slandered woman from the accusation and to demonstrate that those who blame her are lying, and both to show what is true and to put a stop to their ignorance.

That the woman who is the subject of this speech was pre-eminent among 3 pre-eminent men and women, by birth and descent, is not obscure to even a few. It is clear that her mother was Leda, and her actual father was a god and her reputed father a mortal, Tyndareos and Zeus, of whom the one was believed to be because he was and the other was reputed to be because he said he was, and the one was the best of men and the other the master of all. Born of such parents, 4 she had godlike beauty, which she acquired and had openly. In very many she created very strong amorous desires; with a single body she brought together many bodies of men who had great pride for great reasons; some of them had great amounts of wealth, others fame of ancient nobility, others vigour of personal strength, others power of acquired wisdom; and they all came because of a love which wished to conquer and a wish for honour which was unconquered. Who fulfilled his love by obtaining Helen, and why, and how, I shall 5 not say; for to tell those who know what they know carries conviction but does not give pleasure. Passing over now in my speech that former time, I shall proceed to the beginning of my intended speech, and I shall propound the causes which made it reasonable for Helen's departure to Troy to occur.

6　Ἡ γὰρ Τύχης βουλήμασι καὶ θεῶν βουλεύμασι καὶ Ἀνάγκης ψηφίσμασιν ἔπραξεν ἃ ἔπραξεν, ἢ βίᾳ ἁρπασθεῖσα, ἢ λόγοις πεισθεῖσα, <ἢ ἔρωτι ἁλοῦσα>. εἰ μὲν οὖν διὰ τὸ πρῶτον, ἄξιος αἰτιᾶσθαι ὁ αἰτιώμενος· θεοῦ γὰρ προθυμίαν ἀνθρωπίνη προμηθίᾳ ἀδύνατον κωλύειν. πέφυκε γὰρ οὐ τὸ κρεῖσσον ὑπὸ τοῦ ἥσσονος κωλύεσθαι, ἀλλὰ τὸ ἧσσον ὑπὸ τοῦ κρείσσονος ἄρχεσθαι καὶ ἄγεσθαι, καὶ τὸ μὲν κρεῖσσον ἡγεῖσθαι, τὸ δὲ ἧσσον ἕπεσθαι. θεὸς δ᾽ ἀνθρώπου κρεῖσσον καὶ βίᾳ καὶ σοφίᾳ καὶ τοῖς ἄλλοις. εἰ οὖν τῇ Τύχῃ καὶ τῷ θεῷ τὴν αἰτίαν ἀναθετέον, ἢ τὴν Ἑλένην τῆς δυσκλείας ἀπολυτέον.

7　Εἰ δὲ βίᾳ ἡρπάσθη καὶ ἀνόμως ἐβιάσθη καὶ ἀδίκως ὑβρίσθη, δῆλον ὅτι ὁ ἁρπάσας ἢ ὑβρίσας ἠδίκησεν, ἡ δὲ ἁρπασθεῖσα ἢ ὑβρισθεῖσα ἐδυστύχησεν. ἄξιος οὖν ὁ μὲν ἐπιχειρήσας βάρβαρος βάρβαρον ἐπιχείρημα καὶ λόγῳ καὶ νόμῳ καὶ ἔργῳ λόγῳ μὲν αἰτίας, νόμῳ δὲ ἀτιμίας, ἔργῳ δὲ ζημίας τυχεῖν· ἡ δὲ βιασθεῖσα καὶ τῆς πατρίδος στερηθεῖσα καὶ τῶν φίλων ὀρφανισθεῖσα πῶς οὐκ ἂν εἰκότως ἐλεηθείη μᾶλλον ἢ κακολογηθείη; ὁ μὲν γὰρ ἔδρασε δεινά, ἡ δὲ ἔπαθε· δίκαιον οὖν τὴν μὲν οἰκτίρειν, τὸν δὲ μισῆσαι.

8　Εἰ δὲ λόγος ὁ πείσας καὶ τὴν ψυχὴν ἀπατήσας, οὐδὲ πρὸς τοῦτο χαλεπὸν ἀπολογήσασθαι καὶ τὴν αἰτίαν ἀπολύσασθαι ὧδε. λόγος δυνάστης μέγας ἐστίν, ὃς σμικροτάτῳ σώματι καὶ ἀφανεστάτῳ θειότατα ἔργα ἀποτελεῖ· δύναται γὰρ καὶ φόβον παῦσαι καὶ λύπην ἀφελεῖν καὶ χαρὰν ἐνεργάσασθαι καὶ ἔλεον ἐπαυξῆσαι. ταῦτα δὲ

9　ὡς οὕτως ἔχει δείξω· δεῖ δὲ καὶ δόξῃ δεῖξαι τοῖς ἀκούουσι. Τὴν ποίησιν ἅπασαν καὶ νομίζω καὶ ὀνομάζω λόγον ἔχοντα μέτρον· ἧς τοὺς ἀκούοντας εἰσῆλθε καὶ φρίκη περίφοβος καὶ ἔλεος πολύδακρυς καὶ πόθος φιλοπενθής, ἐπ᾽ ἀλλοτρίων τε πραγμάτων καὶ σωμάτων εὐτυχίαις καὶ δυσπραγίαις ἴδιόν τι πάθημα διὰ τῶν λόγων ἔπαθεν ἡ ψυχή.

10　Φέρε δὴ πρὸς ἄλλον ἀπ᾽ ἄλλου μεταστῶ λόγον. αἱ γὰρ ἔνθεοι διὰ λόγων ἐπῳδαὶ ἐπαγωγοὶ ἡδονῆς, ἀπαγωγοὶ λύπης γίγνονται· συγγιγνομένη γὰρ τῇ δόξῃ τῆς ψυχῆς ἡ δύναμις τῆς ἐπῳδῆς ἔθελξε καὶ ἔπεισε καὶ μετέστησεν αὐτὴν γοητείᾳ. γοητείας δὲ καὶ μαγείας δισσαὶ τέχναι εὕρηνται, αἵ εἰσι ψυχῆς ἁμαρτήματα καὶ δόξης ἀπατήματα.

11　Ὅσοι δὲ ὅσους περὶ ὅσων καὶ ἔπεισαν καὶ πείθουσι δὲ ψευδῆ λόγον πλάσαντες. εἰ μὲν γὰρ πάντες περὶ πάντων εἶχον τῶν παροιχομένων μνήμην τῶν τε παρόντων <ἔννοιαν> τῶν τε μελλόντων

22

Either it was because of the wishes of Chance and the purposes of the gods   6
and the decrees of Necessity that she did what she did, or because she was seized
by force, or persuaded by speeches, <or captivated by love>. Now, if it was
because of the first, the accuser deserves to be accused; for it is impossible to
hinder a god's predetermination by human preconsideration. It is not natural for
the stronger to be hindered by the weaker, but for the weaker to be governed
and guided by the stronger, and for the stronger to lead and the weaker to follow.
A god is a stronger thing than a human being, both in force and in wisdom and
in other respects. So if the responsibility is to be attributed to Chance and God,
Helen is to be released from the infamy.

But if she was seized by force and unlawfully violated and unjustly assaulted,   7
clearly the man who seized or assaulted did wrong, and the woman who was
seized or was assaulted suffered misfortune. So the barbarian who undertook a
barbaric undertaking in speech and in law and in deed deserves to receive
accusation in speech, debarment in law, and punishment in deed; but the woman
who was violated and deprived of her country and bereaved of her family, would
she not reasonably be pitied rather than reviled? He performed terrible acts, she
suffered them; so it is just to sympathize with her but to hate him.

But if it was speech that persuaded and deceived her mind, it is also not   8
difficult to make a defence for that and to dispel the accusation thus. Speech is
a powerful ruler. Its substance is minute and invisible, but its achievements are
superhuman; for it is able to stop fear and to remove sorrow and to create joy
and to augment pity. I shall prove that this is so; I must also prove it by opinion   9
to my hearers.

All poetry I consider and call speech with metre. Into those who hear it comes
fearful fright and tearful pity and mournful longing, and at the successes and
failures of others' affairs and persons the mind suffers, through speeches, a
suffering of its own.

Now then, let me move from one speech to another. Inspired incantations   10
through speeches are inducers of pleasure and reducers of sorrow; by inter-
course with the mind's belief, the power of the incantation enchants and
persuades and moves it by sorcery. Two arts of sorcery and magic have been
invented; they are deviations of mind and deceptions of belief.

How many men have persuaded and do persuade how many, on how many   11
subjects, by fabricating false speech! For if everyone, on every subject, possessed memory of the past and <understanding> of the present and foreknowl-

πρόνοιαν, οὐκ ἂν ὁμοίως †ὅμοιος† ἦν ὁ λόγος· ἀλλὰ νῦν γε οὔτε μνησθῆναι τὸ παροιχόμενον οὔτε σκέψασθαι τὸ παρὸν οὔτε μαντεύσασθαι τὸ μέλλον εὐπόρως ἔχει, ὥστε περὶ τῶν πλείστων οἱ πλεῖστοι τὴν δόξαν σύμβουλον τῇ ψυχῇ παρέχονται. ἡ δὲ δόξα σφαλερὰ καὶ ἀβέβαιος οὖσα σφαλεραῖς καὶ ἀβεβαίοις εὐτυχίαις
12 περιβάλλει τοὺς αὐτῇ χρωμένους. τίς οὖν αἰτία κωλύει καὶ τὴν Ἑλένην †ὕμνος ἦλθεν ὁμοίως ἂν οὐ νέαν οὖσαν ὥσπερ εἰ βιατήριον βίᾳ ἡρπάσθη; τὸ γὰρ τῆς πειθοῦς ἐξῆν ὁ δὲ νοῦς καίτοι εἰ ἀνάγκη ὁ εἰδὼς ἕξει μὲν οὖν†, τὴν δὲ δύναμιν τὴν αὐτὴν ἔχει. λόγος γὰρ ψυχὴν ὁ πείσας ἣν ἔπεισεν ἠνάγκασε καὶ πείθεσθαι τοῖς λεγομένοις καὶ συναινέσαι τοῖς ποιουμένοις. ὁ μὲν οὖν πείσας ὡς ἀναγκάσας ἀδικεῖ, ἡ δὲ πεισθεῖσα ὡς ἀναγκασθεῖσα τῷ λόγῳ μάτην ἀκούει κακῶς.
13 Ὅτι δ' ἡ πειθὼ προσιοῦσα τῷ λόγῳ καὶ τὴν ψυχὴν ἐτυπώσατο ὅπως ἐβούλετο, χρὴ μαθεῖν πρῶτον μὲν τοὺς τῶν μετεωρολόγων λόγους, οἵτινες δόξαν ἀντὶ δόξης τὴν μὲν ἀφελόμενοι τὴν δ' ἐνεργασάμενοι τὰ ἄπιστα καὶ ἄδηλα φαίνεσθαι τοῖς τῆς δόξης ὄμμασιν ἐποίησαν· δεύτερον δὲ τοὺς ἀναγκαίους διὰ λόγων ἀγῶνας, ἐν οἷς εἷς λόγος πολὺν ὄχλον ἔτερψε καὶ ἔπεισε τέχνῃ γραφείς, οὐκ ἀληθείᾳ λεχθείς· τρίτον <δὲ> φιλοσόφων λόγων ἀμίλλας, ἐν αἷς δείκνυται καὶ γνώμης τάχος ὡς εὐμετάβολον ποιοῦν τὴν τῆς δόξης
14 πίστιν. τὸν αὐτὸν δὲ λόγον ἔχει ἥ τε τοῦ λόγου δύναμις πρὸς τὴν τῆς ψυχῆς τάξιν ἥ τε τῶν φαρμάκων τάξις πρὸς τὴν τῶν σωμάτων φύσιν. ὥσπερ γὰρ τῶν φαρμάκων ἄλλους ἄλλα χυμοὺς ἐκ τοῦ σώματος ἐξάγει, καὶ τὰ μὲν νόσου τὰ δὲ βίου παύει, οὕτω καὶ τῶν λόγων οἱ μὲν ἐλύπησαν, οἱ δὲ ἔτερψαν, οἱ δὲ ἐφόβησαν, οἱ δὲ εἰς θάρσος κατέστησαν τοὺς ἀκούοντας, οἱ δὲ πειθοῖ τινι κακῇ τὴν ψυχὴν ἐξεφαρμάκευσαν καὶ ἐγοήτευσαν.
15 Καὶ ὅτι μέν, εἰ λόγῳ ἐπείσθη, οὐκ ἠδίκησεν ἀλλ' ἠτύχησεν, εἴρηται· τὴν δὲ τετάρτην αἰτίαν τῷ τετάρτῳ λόγῳ διέξειμι. εἰ γὰρ ἔρως ἦν ὁ ταῦτα πάντα πράξας, οὐ χαλεπῶς διαφεύξεται τὴν τῆς λεγομένης γεγονέναι ἁμαρτίας αἰτίαν. ἃ γὰρ ὁρῶμεν, ἔχει φύσιν οὐχ ἣν ἡμεῖς θέλομεν, ἀλλ' ἣν ἕκαστον ἔτυχε· διὰ δὲ τῆς ὄψεως ἡ
16 ψυχὴ κἂν τοῖς τρόποις τυποῦται. αὐτίκα γάρ, ὅταν πολέμια σώματα καὶ πολέμιον ἐπὶ πολεμίᾳ ὁπλίσει κόσμον χαλκοῦ καὶ σιδήρου, τοῦ μὲν ἀλεξητήριον τοῦ δὲ προβλήματα, ἐπιθεάσηται ἡ ὄψις, ἐταράχθη καὶ ἐτάραξε τὴν ψυχήν, ὥστε πολλάκις κινδύνου τοῦ μέλλοντος <ὡς> ὄντος φεύγουσιν ἐκπλαγέντες· ἰσχυρὰ γὰρ ἡ ἀμέλεια τοῦ νόμου

24

edge of the future, speech would not be equally <powerful>; but as it is, neither remembering a past event nor investigating a present one nor prophesying a future one is easy, so that on most subjects most men make belief their mind's adviser. But belief, being slippery and unreliable, brings slippery and unreliable success to those who employ it. So what reason is there against Helen's also 12 <having come under the influence of speech just as much against her will as if she had been seized by violence of violators? For persuasion expelled sense; and indeed persuasion, though not having an appearance of compulsion,> has the same power. For speech, the persuader, compelled mind, the persuaded, both to obey what was said and to approve what was done. So the persuader, because he compelled, is guilty; but the persuaded, because she was compelled by his speech, is wrongly reproached.

To show that persuasion, when added to speech, also moulds the mind in the 13 way it wishes, one should note first the speeches of astronomers, who substituting belief for belief, demolishing one and establishing another, make the incredible and obscure become clear to the eyes of belief; and secondly compulsory contests conducted by means of speeches, in which a single speech pleases and persuades a large crowd, because written with skill, not spoken with truth; <and> thirdly conflicts of philosophical speeches, in which it is shown that quick-wittedness too makes the opinion which is based on belief changeable. The power of speech bears the same relation to the ordering of the mind 14 as the ordering of drugs bears to the constitution of bodies. Just as different drugs expel different humours from the body, and some stop it from being ill but others stop it from living, so too some speeches cause sorrow, some cause pleasure, some cause fear, some give the hearers confidence, some drug and bewitch the mind with an evil persuasion.

That, if she was persuaded by speech, it was not a misdeed but a mischance, 15 has been stated; and I shall examine the fourth cause in the fourth part of my speech. If it was love that brought all this about, she will without difficulty escape the accusation of the offence said to have been committed. Things that we see do not have the nature which we wish them to have but the nature which each of them actually has; and by seeing them the mind is moulded in its character too. For instance, when the sight surveys hostile persons and a hostile 16 array of bronze and iron for hostile armament, offensive array of the one and shields of the other, it is alarmed, and it alarms the mind, so that often people flee in panic when some danger is imminent as if it were present. So strong is

διὰ τὸν φόβον εἰσῳκίσθη τὸν ἀπὸ τῆς ὄψεως, ἥτις ἐλθοῦσα ἐποίησεν ἀμελῆσαι καὶ τοῦ καλοῦ τοῦ διὰ τῶν αόμον κρινομένου καὶ τοῦ
17 ἀγαθοῦ τοῦ διὰ τὴν δίκην γιγνομένου. ἤδη δέ τινες ἰδόντες φοβερὰ καὶ τοῦ παρόντος ἐν τῷ παρόντι χρόνῳ φρονήματος ἐξέστησαν· οὕτως ἀπέσβεσε καὶ ἐξήλασεν ὁ φόβος τὸ νόημα. πολλοὶ δὲ ματαίοις πόνοις καὶ δειναῖς νόσοις καὶ δυσιάτοις μανίαις περιέπεσον· οὕτως εἰκόνας τῶν ὁρωμένων πραγμάτων ἡ ὄψις ἐνέγραψεν ἐν τῷ φρονήματι. καὶ τὰ μὲν δειματοῦντα πολλὰ μὲν παραλείπεται, ὅμοια δ' ἐστὶ τὰ παραλειπόμενα οἷάπερ <τὰ> λεγόμενα.
18 Ἀλλὰ μὴν οἱ γραφεῖς ὅταν ἐκ πολλῶν χρωμάτων καὶ σωμάτων ἓν σῶμα καὶ σχῆμα τελείως ἀπεργάσωνται, τέρπουσι τὴν ὄψιν. ἡ δὲ τῶν ἀνδριάντων ποίησις καὶ ἡ τῶν ἀγαλμάτων ἐργασία νόσον ἡδεῖαν παρέσχετο τοῖς ἄμμασιν. οὕτω τὰ μὲν λυπεῖν, τὰ δὲ τέρπειν πέφυκε τὴν ὄψιν. πολλὰ δὲ πολλοῖς πολλῶν ἔρωτα καὶ πόθον
19 ἐνεργάζεται πραγμάτων καὶ σωμάτων. εἰ οὖν τῷ τοῦ Ἀλεξάνδρου σώματι τὸ τῆς Ἑλένης ὄμμα ἡσθὲν προθυμίαν καὶ ἅμιλλαν ἔρωτος τῇ ψυχῇ παρέδωκε, τί θαυμαστόν; ὃς εἰ μὲν θεός, ἔχων θείαν δύναμιν, πῶς ἂν ὁ ἥσσων εἴη τοῦτον ἀπώσασθαι καὶ ἀμύνασθαι δυνατός; εἰ δ' ἐστὶν ἀνθρώπινον νόσημα καὶ ψυχῆς ἀγνόημαμ, οὐχ ὡς ἁμάρτημα μεμπτέον ἀλλ' ὡς ἀτύχημα νομιστέον· ἦλθε γάρ, ὡς ἦλθε, ψυχῆς ἀγρεύμασιν, οὐ γνώμης βουλεύμασι, καὶ ἔρωτος ἀνάγκαις, οὐ τέχνης παρασκευαῖς.
20 Πῶς οὖν χρὴ δίκαιον ἡγήσασθαι τὸν τῆς Ἑλένης μῶμον; ἥτις, εἴτε <ὄψει> ἐρασθεῖσα εἴτε λόγῳ πεισθεῖσα εἴτε βίᾳ ἁρπασθεῖσα εἴτε ὑπὸ θείας ἀνάγκης ἀναγκασθεῖσα ἔπραξεν ἃ ἔπραξε, πάντως διαφεύγει τὴν αἰτίαν.
21 Ἀφεῖλον τῷ λόγῳ δύσκλειαν γυναικός, ἐνέμεινα τῇ γνώμῃ ἣν ἐθέμην ἐν ἀρχῇ τοῦ λόγου· ἐπειράθην καταλῦσαι μώμου ἀδικίαν καὶ δόξης ἀμαθίαν, ἐβουλήθην γράψαι τὸν λόγον Ἑλένης μὲν ἐγκώμιον, ἐμὸν δὲ παίγνιον.

the disregard of law which is implanted in them because of the fear caused by the sight; when it befalls, it makes them disregard both the honour which is awarded for obeying the law and the benefit which accrues for doing right. And 17
some people before now, on seeing frightful things, have also lost their presence of mind at the present moment; fear so extinguishes and expels thought. And many have fallen into groundless distress and terrible illness and incurable madness; so deeply does sight engrave on the mind images of actions that are seen. And as far as frightening things are concerned, many are omitted, but those omitted are similar to those mentioned.

But when painters complete out of many colours and objects a single object 18
and form, they please the sight. The making of figures and the creation of statues provides a pleasant disease for the eyes. Thus some things naturally give distress and others pleasure to the sight. Many things create in many people love and desire of many actions and bodies. So if Helen's eye, pleased by Alexander's 19
body, transmitted an eagerness and striving of love to her mind, what is surprising? If love is a god with a god's power, how would the weaker be able to repel and resist it? But if it is a human malady and incapacity of mind, it should not be blamed as an impropriety but considered as an adversity; for it comes, when it does come, through deceptions of mind, not intentions of thought, and through compulsions of love, not contrivances of skill.

So how should one consider the blame of Helen just? Whether she did what 20
she did because she was enamoured <by sight> or persuaded by speech or seized by force or compelled by divine necessity, in every case she escapes the accusation.

I have removed by my speech a woman's infamy, I have kept to the purpose 21
which I set myself at the start of my speech; I attempted to dispel injustice of blame and ignorance of belief, I wished to write the speech as an encomium of Helen and an amusement for myself.

Commentary

1 Gorgias has clearly taken special care with his opening sentences. He regards it as his first duty to state the object of his speech, and he does this by stating a general aim to which his speech makes an individual contribution: 'one should praise what is praiseworthy and blame what is blameworthy; so I shall now show that it is wrong to blame Helen.' But the general statement is cast in the form of lists of parallel words and phrases linked by μέν and δέ in a characteristically Gorgianic manner.

κόσμος (sc. ἐστί): 'goodness', 'merit', the thing which brings renown, the proper condition in virtue of which a city is a good city, a body is a good body, etc. (Not 'ornament' here, because it is the good order of the thing itself, not an extraneous addition; cf. Bona in *Riv. Fil.* 102 [1974] 5-6.) For this sense cf. Thucydides 1.5.2: robbery is still a way of life for some backward peoples, 'who regard it as a merit to do this well', οἷς κόσμος καλῶς τοῦτο δρᾶν.

εὐανδρία: 'excellence of its men', rather than LSJ's 'abundance'; εὐ- indicates quality rather than quantity.

ἀρετή: one might have supposed that ἀρετή just meant 'merit', virtually equivalent to κόσμος. But it is in accordance with the archaic use of the word to regard it as applicable primarily to action.

ἀλήθεια: truth is the most important virtue in speech. Notice that Gorgias does not say (though some critics, beginning with Plato *Phaidros* 267a, have tried to make him say it) that telling the truth is less important than convincing the hearer. Convincing and entertaining are the two reasons for speaking (cf. 5 πίστιν...τέρψιν), but it is discreditable if truth is sacrificed to attain these ends.

ἀκοσμία: 'a disgrace', the opposite of κόσμος.

ἄνδρα...πρᾶγμα: some of these nouns are the same as in the previous sentence, others not. There seems to be no significant distinction between ἔργον and πρᾶγμα: probably Gorgias' only reason for including both was to achieve an even number of items in his list.

μῶμον: generally poetic; the usual word for 'blame' in later prose is ὄνειδος.

2 τοῦ αὐτοῦ ἀνδρός: 'it is the part of the same man to...' means that the

28

general task of saying what ought to be said includes, as a particular instance, refutation of Helen's critics.

ἐλέγξαι: Dobree suggested that some words were missing here, and Diels suggested that the sense was ἐλέγξαι τὸ λεγόμενον οὐκ ὀρθῶς· προσήκει τοίνυν ἐλέγξαι...: the loss would be explained by haplography. But no supplement is really necessary; the sense and construction are satisfactory without it, and it is not for us to foist on Gorgias yet another redundant antithesis.

ὁμόψυχος, 'with the same mind', 'unanimous', seems to occur only here in classical Greek. (In Diodoros 15.53.3 it is generally emended to ὁμόψηφον.) Gorgias may have coined it to make a word similar in sound to ὁμόφωνος.

ἥ τε τῶν ποιητῶν ἀκουσάντων πίστις: 'both the belief of those who have listened to poets'. This (the manuscripts' text) seems possible, though several editors have wished to emend to produce a more antithetical expression e.g. ἥ τε τῶν ποιητῶν <πύστις ἥ τε τῶν> ἀκουσάντων πίστις (Immisch). Others, retaining the manuscripts' original reading, make ἀκουσάντων agree with ποιητῶν, 'poets who have heard', meaning either poets who have been inspired by the Muses (Segal in *HSCP* 66 [1962] 145 n.63, following Norden) or poets who have inherited an oral tradition from earlier poets (Bona in *Riv. Fil.* 102 [1974] 30 n.1); but I do not believe that ἀκουσάντων can convey either of those meanings without a genitive to denote the source of what is heard.

φήμη: 'omen', 'significant sound'. Helen's name seems to be a symbol of the disasters of the Trojan War, because it sounds like ἑλεῖν, 'destroy'. Gorgias probably has in mind the famous lyric of Aiskhylos *Agamemnon* 681ff.: τίς ποτ᾽ ὠνόμαζεν ὧδ᾽ ἐς τὸ πᾶν ἐτητύμως...Ἑλέναν; ἐπεὶ πρεπόντως ἑλέ-νας, ἕλανδρος, ἑλέπτολις..., 'Who named her Helen, with such entire truth? For fittingly ship-destroying, man-destroying, city-destroying...'.

τῶν συμφορῶν μνήμη: the rhyme of φήμη and μνήμη is exploited also in Lysias 2.3 μνήμην παρὰ τῆς φήμης λαβών. Gorgias produces a pair of parallel phrases by adding a genitive to each, but the parallelism of construction is artificial, because τοῦ ὀνόματος is a subjective genitive (Helen's name does the speaking) but τῶν συμφορῶν is an objective genitive (the calamities are what it recalls). Other places where he uses one subjective and one objective genitive to produce a pair of phrases which sound parallel are 10 ψυχῆς ἁμαρτήματα καὶ δόξης ἀπατήματα, 19 ψυχῆς ἀγρεύμασιν, οὐ γνώμης βουλεύμασι, and there is another combination of different kinds of genitive in 3 ὁ μὲν ἀνδρῶν κράτιστος, ὁ δὲ πάντων τύραννος.

λογισμόν τινα τῷ λόγῳ δούς: 'putting some reasoning into my speech' or 'contributing some logic to the discussion'. Some scholars have read too much into this phrase. Verdenius (in *The Sophists and their Legacy* 117) translates 'a special kind of argument'; but τινα does not mean 'a special kind of'. Kerferd (*The Sophistic Movement* 81) writes 'what Gorgias seems to be saying is that in order to get at the truth it is necessary to indicate the truth or reality itself and not the logos'; but I cannot find that in the Greek text.

κακῶς ἀκούουσαν: 'having a bad reputation'.

δεῖξαί τε τάληθὲς καὶ: this seems the best restoration of a textually corrupt phrase; cf. MacDowell in *CQ* 11 (1961) 120-1.

3 Gorgias begins his account of Helen from the beginning, by starting with her birth.

τὰ πρῶτα: neuter plural used of one person (like colloquial English 'the tops'): cf. Herodotus 6.100.3 Αἰσχίνης ὁ Νόθωνος ἐὼν τῶν Ἐρετριέων τὰ πρῶτα, 'Aiskhines the son of Nothon, who was the leading man in Eretria', 9.78.1, Aristophanes *Frogs* 421.

οὐκ ἄδηλον οὐδὲ ὀλίγοις: by repetition of οὐ Gorgias makes a balanced phrase out of even so simple a statement as 'everyone knows'.

μητρός: sc. ἦν: 'she was the daughter of…'. In the legend Leda was the wife of Tyndareos, king of Sparta; Zeus came to her disguised as a swan, and she subsequently gave birth to Helen and Klytaimestra, Kastor and Polydeukes.

ἐλέχθη: the reading of late manuscripts, perhaps merely a medieval conjecture, but it must be preferred to the oldest manuscripts' ἠλέγχθη, which does not make sense; cf. *CQ* 11 (1961) 121.

4 ὃ λαβοῦσα καὶ οὐ λαθοῦσα ἔσχε : 'and when she acquired it, it was certainly no secret that she had got it'. If καὶ is right (some editors delete it), it is not connective but emphasizes οὐ λαθοῦσα. One might have expected εἶχε it is not clear why Gorgias here, and again towards the end of 4, prefers the aorist to the imperfect of this verb.

ἔρωτος: a defining genitive (not the objective genitive usual with ἐπιθυμία): 'amorous desires'.

ἐνηργάσατο: in the classical period ἐργάζομαι has ἠργ- in the imperfect and aorist, εἰργ- in the perfect; cf. Meisterhans *Grammatik der attischen Inschriften*[3] 171.

συνήγαγεν: many men came to Sparta as her suitors.

μεγέθη: 'large amounts'. This concrete plural use of μέγεθος is uncommon, but cf. Plato *Protagoras* 356c φαίνεται ὑμῖν τῇ ὄψει τὰ αὐτὰ μεγέθη ἐγγύθεν μὲν μείζω, πόρρωθεν δὲ ἐλάττω, 'the same magnitudes appear larger to you when seen from near by, and smaller from a distance'.

5 In 3 and 4 it seemed as if Gorgias were going to give a biographical account

of Helen. But now he breaks that off, on the ground that her story is too well known to need telling, and he turns instead to a logical analysis of her possible reasons for eloping with Paris.

ὅστις...: Menelaos married Helen and succeeded Tyndareos as king of Sparta.

πίστιν...τέρψιν: to convince and to entertain are the two objects of speech. Telling a story which the listeners already know achieves the first but not the second. For πίστιν ἔχει with a story or statement as subject cf. Euripides *Elektra* 737-8, Aristotle *Nikomakheian Ethics* 1179a 17-18.

ὑπερβάς: 'skipping' (not 'going over'). Notice the interlacing: τὸν τότε goes with τὸν χρόνον while τῷ λόγῳ goes with νῦν ὑπερβάς .

εἰκός: 'reasonable', i.e. not to be condemned as wrong.

6   Gorgias first lists all four possible reasons for Helen's elopement, before proceeding to discuss each in turn. The first reason is expressed by three phrases (each being a dative plural noun with a genitive), the other three by one phrase each (a participle with a dative), so as to produce symmetry: three phrases precede and three follow the central ἔπραξεν ἃ ἔπραξεν.

Τύχης βουλήμασι καὶ θεῶν βουλεύμασι: blaming the gods was an old way of defending Helen; cf. *Iliad* 3.164, where Priam says to Helen οὔ τί μοι αἰτίη ἐσσί, θεοί νύ μοι αἴτιοί εἰσιν, 'I do not blame you, I blame the gods'. Chance is a goddess with wishes of her own; cf. Pindar *Olympian Odes* 12.1-2, Sophokles *Antigone* 1158, Menander *Aspis* 147-8, and Demosthenes *Epistles* 2.5 τῆς δ' ἀναγκαίας μέν, ἀγνώμονος δὲ Τύχης οὐχ ὡς δίκαιον ἦν, ἀλλ' ὡς ἐβούλετο, κρινάσης τὸν ὑπὲρ τῆς τῶν Ἑλλήνων ἐλευθερίας ἀγῶνα, 'when Chance, irresistible and inconsiderate, decided the contest for the freedom of Greece, not as was right but as she wished'.

Ἀνάγκης ψηφίσμασιν: Gorgias is said to have been a pupil of Empedokles (Diogenes Laertios 8.58, *Souda* γ 388), and so his phrase may possibly be a reminiscence of the line ἔστιν Ἀνάγκης χρῆμα, θεῶν ψήφισμα παλαιόν, 'there is an oracle of Necessity, an ancient decree of the gods' (Empedokles 115). Other classical Greek authors do not generally personify Necessity, and they seldom use the word ψήφισμα for decisions of gods (though there is an instance in Aristophanes *Wasps* 378).

<ἢ ἔρωτι ἁλοῦσα>: a medieval conjecture. 15 shows that Gorgias must have written some such phrase at this point.

αἰτιᾶσθαι: passive.

ἀπολυτέον: 'one must release' (not 'acquit', as LSJ say, for δύσκλεια is a burden, not an alleged offence).

7   βάρβαρος: non-Greek. βάρβαρον: brutal.

καὶ λόγῳ καὶ νόμῳ καὶ ἔργῳ: with ἐπιχειρήσας. The three ways of effecting an action are by doing it oneself (ἔργῳ), by telling someone to do it (λόγῳ), and by making a law or rule requiring it to be done (νόμῳ). The use of καὶ does not mean that Paris actually used all three methods (he can hardly have used νόμος); it is just 'by any possible means', just as δικαίως καὶ ἀδίκως means 'by fair means or foul'. Cf. the oath quoted in Andokides 1.97: κτενῶ καὶ λόγῳ καὶ ἔργῳ καὶ ψήφῳ καὶ τῇ ἐμαυτοῦ χειρί, ἂν δυνατὸς ὦ, ὃς ἂν καταλύσῃ τὴν δημοκρατίαν, 'I shall kill both by word and by deed and by vote and by my own hand, if I can, anyone who overthrows the democracy'.

λόγῳ μὲν...: the same three datives are repeated. Gorgias' sense of antithesis naturally requires the punishment to fit the crime.

ἀτιμίας: 'loss of rights'. In early times this meant 'outlawry', later just 'disfranchisement'; but Gorgias is not concerned with legal technicalities, which are hardly applicable to a legend.

τῶν φίλων: 'her dear ones', meaning her family, not merely friends.

8 δυνάστης: a striking personification. Compare Euripides *Hecuba* 814-19, where πειθώ is a τύραννος (and everyone should pay fees to learn it, a passage which has been taken as an advertisement for Gorgias; cf. M. Tierney's note ad loc.).

σώματι: Greeks sometimes talk about speech as if it were a physical object, so small that it cannot be seen, flying from one person to another; compare Homer's 'winged words' (ἔπεα πτερόεντα). For Gorgias this may be just a figure of speech, part of the personification of speech as a ruler; it is not safe to deduce from it that he really believed that speech was a material substance.

παῦσαι...ἀφελεῖν...ἐνεργάσασθαι...ἐπαυξῆσαι: The verbs are varied for the sake of rhetorical balance, not because of any difference of meaning between the first two or between the second two.

9 δόξῃ: 'by opinion' is strange; no explanation or emendation so far suggested is quite convincing. δείγμασι δεῖξαι, 'to prove it by examples', would give perfect sense and a Gorgianic sound, but it is not clear why that should have been corrupted to δόξῃ δεῖξαι.

τὴν ποίησιν...: no connective particle, because this sentence begins the proof foreshadowed by δείξω in the previous sentence. The proof consists of adducing different kinds of speech as examples: first poetry, then magical incantations.

λόγον ἔχοντα μέτρον: Aristotle in the first chapter of his *Poetics* gives a more complex analysis; he says that the media of poetry are λόγος, ῥυθμός, and ἁρμονία (speech, rhythm, and melody), and he uses the term μέτρον to mean λόγος combined with ῥυθμός. But this distinction is of no importance to

Gorgias, whose concern at this point is only to establish that poetry involves λόγος. Scholars who object that poetical style differs from oratorical style are making too much of the passage; Gorgias does not here enter into the question of style, but is just saying – what is undeniably true – that poetry, like oratory, uses words. Nor does he say anything here about the source of poetic inspiration. J. de Romilly (*JHS* 93 [1973] 155-62) infers that he regards poetry as a human τέχνη, not divinely inspired; but the inference is shaky, because the words ἔνθεοι and τέχναι in 10 show that, for Gorgias, a τέχνη is not incompatible with divine inspiration.

εἰσῆλθε: 'enters', aorist for a regular occurrence; so also are the other aorist indicatives in 9 and 10. The nominative words which follow are carefully equalized in length.

περίφοβος: this adjective normally qualifies a person, but another passage where it may perhaps qualify terror, as here, is Aiskhylos *Suppliants* 736 περίφοβόν μ' ἔχει τάρβος 'fearful terror grips me'. The mention of fear and pity aroused by poetry naturally reminds us of Aristotle *Poetics* 1449b 27, but Gorgias does not anticipate Aristotle's theory of κάθαρσις.

πόθος: longing for a person absent or dead.

φιλοπενθής: 'indulging in grief'. The word seems to occur nowhere else before Plutarch.

ἐπ' governs εὐτυχίαις καὶ δυσπραγίαις.

φέρε δή...λόγον: part of 9, according to the traditional numbering; but clearly it ought to be regarded as the start of a new paragraph.

πρὸς ἄλλον...λόγον: possibly 'to another part of my speech' (cf. 15 τῷ τετάρτῳ λόγῳ), but more probably 'to another variety of speech' as an example to support the argument. After poetry, Gorgias' next instance of a powerful type of speech is spells and other magical utterances. Magic, like poetry, produces emotional effects. But that does not mean that poetry is a kind of magic, or vice versa; the connection between them is somewhat overstated by J. de Romilly *Magic and Rhetoric* ch. 1. Gorgias' ἄλλον ἀπ' ἄλλου makes clear that he regards them as two distinct examples in his argument.

10 ἔνθεοι διὰ λόγων ἐπῳδαί: 'inspired incantations using words', charms which induce a person to believe or to do something contrary to his previous belief or intention. Gorgias accepts the popular belief that spells have this power, and he contrives to give the credit for their effectiveness to words while at the same time accepting the popular view that their effectiveness is derived from the gods.

γοητείας δὲ καὶ μαγείας: the two genitives define the two τέχναι: i.e. 'there exists an art of sorcery and an art of magic'. Gorgias does not indicate what he thinks is the difference between them. Some scholars have supposed that the διϲϲαὶ τέχναι are two techniques possessed by the arts of sorcery and magic, and have proceeded to make guesses at the identity of the techniques, e.g. corruption and illusion, or prose and verse. But this is unlikely; if Gorgias had meant this, he would have given some sort of definition or indication of what the two techniques were.

ψυχῆς ἁμαρτήματα καὶ δόξης ἀπατήματα: the two arts mislead the mind and deceive the judgement. ψυχῆς ἁμαρτήματα and δόξης ἀπατήματα make a rhyming pair of the kind which Gorgias likes, and that, for him, is a good enough reason to put both phrases in; so we need not suppose that there is any significant difference of meaning, still less that one belongs to γοητεία only and the other to μαγεία only.

11 ὅϲοι δὲ ὅϲουϲ περὶ ὅϲων: an exclamation, 'how many...!' Gorgias just piles one ὅϲοϲ on top of another. Subtler authors employ this kind of exclamatory polyptoton (the use of the same word in different cases) to express a contrast; cf. Sophokles *Ajax* 923 οἷοϲ ὢν οἵωϲ ἔχειϲ, 'so great a man fallen so low!', and *Palatine Anthology* 7.740.6 (an epitaph by Leonidas) γαίηϲ ὅϲϲηϲ ὅϲϲον ἔχει μόριον, 'so small a share of so large an earth!'

καὶ...καὶ...δὲ: 'both...and...too' (Denniston *The Greek Particles* 199-203).

<ἔννοιαν>: Reiske's suggestion; some word like this is clearly required.

ὅμοιοϲ cannot be right. The rhetoric of the antithesis demands that εἰ μὲν γὰρ...ὁ λόγοϲ should express the hypothetical state of affairs which is not the case, by contrast both with the preceding sentence (ὅϲοι...πλάϲαντεϲ) and the following one (ἀλλὰ νῦν γε...παρέχονται) which expresses what actually does happen. The preceding sentence says that many people are persuaded by false speech; so this sentence should say 'If ..., speech would not be similarly persuasive'. Diels-Kranz try to get this sense out of ὅμοιοϲ by interpreting it as *communis*, i.e. 'widespread', but ὅμοιοϲ cannot mean that. Kerferd (*The Sophistic Movement* 81) tries to fit the sentence in with his view of Gorgias' philosophy by making it a statement that speech never reproduces facts: 'if men did possess knowledge, the logos would (visibly) not be similar (to that of which they possess the knowledge)'. The objections to that are: (a) it does not provide the rhetorically necessary contrast with the preceding and following sentences (instead of εἰ μὲν γὰρ πάντεϲ we should want εἰ γὰρ καὶ πάντεϲ, 'for even if everyone did possess knowledge'), (b) the special philosophical point, not mentioned elsewhere in the speech, would not be clear to listeners from the one word ὅμοιοϲ, (c) ὁμοίωϲ is left unexplained, because 'similarly similar' makes no sense. I think that we must reject ὅμοιοϲ as a scribal error, derived from the preceding ὁμοίωϲ. It has

34

ousted a word meaning 'effective' or 'powerful', perhaps δυνατός: cf. 8 δυνάστης, 14 δύναμις, both referring to speech.

ἀλλὰ νῦν γε: 'but as things are', 'but in fact', opposed to the hypothetical condition of εἰ μέν.... The word ἀλλὰ is my conjecture; I previously (CQ 11 [1961] 121) defended the reading ἢ τὰ νῦν γε, but now think that an adversative word is necessary to respond to the preceding μέν. An alternative possibility is νῦν δὲ (Dobree).

εὐπόρως ἔχει: this sentence is misinterpreted by some scholars as meaning that the attainment of knowledge is not possible. In fact it says that the attainment of knowledge is not easy, clearly implying that it is possible.

τὴν δόξαν: when the mind cannot discover the facts by direct apprehension (μνήμη, <ἔννοια>, and πρόνοια, to which μνησθῆναι, σκέψασθαι, and μαντεύσασθαι are equivalent), it falls back on δόξα, which is opinion based on conjecture or hearsay.

σύμβουλον: a notable personification.

παρέχονται: middle voice, 'supply for their own use'.

12 τίς οὖν αἰτία...τὴν αὐτὴν ἔχει: these two sentences are too corrupt in the manuscripts for their exact wording to be restored with any certainty, though the general sense is not in doubt. Among many alternative possibilities my preference is for the following text (which incorporates conjectures by Blass, Croiset, Diels, and myself) τίς οὖν αἰτία κωλύει καὶ τὴν Ἑλένην ὑπὸ λόγους ἐλθεῖν ὁμοίως ἄκουσαν οὖσαν, ὥσπερ εἰ βιατήρων βίᾳ ἡρπάσθη; ὑπὸ γὰρ τῆς πειθοῦς ἐξηλάθη νοῦς· καίτοι πειθὼ ἀνάγκης εἶδος ἔχει μὲν οὔ, τὴν δὲ δύναμιν τὴν αὐτὴν ἔχει. This is the text rendered in my translation.

πείσας...ἔπεισεν...πείθεσθαι: no one English verb will translate all that this verb means. πείθεσθαι is both 'believe' and 'obey', but the antithesis and chiasmus make the latter sense more prominent here: λεγομένοις and συναινέσαι refer to speech, πείθεσθαι and ποιουμένοις to action.

ἀδικεῖ: 'is guilty'. This verb is regularly used in the present with reference to an offence committed in the past, meaning that the guilt still obtains.

μάτην: 'falsely' (LSJ μάτην 3).

13 ὅτι: 'with regard to the fact that', 'for evidence that' (LSJ ὅτι A.IV).

προσιοῦσα: 'added to', 'combined with' (LSJ πρόσειμι 1.5).

ἐτυπώσατο: 'moulds' or 'stamps'. The metaphor is discussed by C.P. Segal in HSCP 66 (1962) 142 n.44. All the past indicative verbs in 13 and 14 denote regular occurrences.

μαθεῖν: 'notice' (LSJ μανθάνω III). Three more kinds of persuasive λόγοι are now listed: those of scientists, law-court speakers, and philosophers.

μετεωρολόγων: 'astronomers', 'cosmologists', such as Thales or Anaxagoras, who argue that the structure of the universe is not as it appears to ordinary people.

τοῖς τῆς δόξης ὄμμασιν: not quite equivalent to the English phrase 'the mind's eye', because δόξα refers to belief rather than imagination. (For the metaphor cf. Plato *Republic* 533d τὸ τῆς ψυχῆς ὄμμα, 'the eye of the soul'.) Different scientists hold different theories, but the ordinary person does not know from his own experience which one is right. Consequently he believes the one which a scientist, by speech, makes clear and plausible to his mind. There is nothing here to support those modern scholars who maintain that Gorgias considers all scientific theories false; he is merely saying that people can be persuaded by speech to believe a particular theory, whether it is false or not.

ἀναγκαίους: the verbal contests here must be those of the law-courts, but two interpretations of ἀναγκαίους have been suggested:

a) 'Under compulsion': the speaker is forced by circumstances to make a persuasive speech, since otherwise he will lose the case. So Diels, comparing Plato *Theaitetos* 172e οὐκ ἐγχωρεῖ περὶ οὗ ἂν ἐπιθυμήσωσι τοὺς λόγους ποιεῖσθαι, ἀλλ᾽ ἀνάγκην ἔχων ὁ ἀντίδικος ἐφέστηκεν, 'it is not possible for them to make their speeches on any subject they wish, but the opposing litigant stands over them and compels them'.

b) 'Compelling', 'persuasive'. So S. Melikoff-Tolstoj (*Philologische Wochenschrift* 49 [1929] 28).

The objection to (b) is that Gorgias maintains that the discourses of scientists and philosophers are also persuasive, so that ἀναγκαίους, if interpreted in this way, fails to distinguish law-court speeches from the kinds of speech mentioned in the other parts of the sentence. I therefore prefer (a). But I suggest that emendation to δικανικοὺς is also worth considering.

εἷς inserted by Gorgias simply to make a contrast with πολὺν ὄχλον.

ἔτερψε καὶ ἔπεισε: cf. 5 πίστιν...τέρψιν.

τέχνῃ γραφείς: 'written with skill'. Notice that Gorgias implies that it is normal for a law-court speech to be written. τέχνη means skill acquired by study or training, such as Gorgias himself provided.

οὐκ ἀληθείᾳ: as with scientific discourse, so also here with legal speeches, Gorgias does not mean that every speech is necessarily untrue, but merely that a speech which is untrue can convince if artfully composed.

λεχθείς, unnecessary for the sense, is added to make a balance of sound with γραφείς.

γνώμης τάχος: it is interesting that Gorgias regards quick thinking as characteristic of philosophers (rather than of scientists or law-court speakers), and associates them with debating rather than lecturing. But there is no ground for thinking that he is referring to Socrates or any other individual in particular.

εὐμετάβολον: cf. 11 σφαλερὰ καὶ ἀβέβαιος. An opinion based merely on belief, not on knowledge, is easily changed by clever speaking.

14 λόγον: 'relation' (LSJ λόγος II.I). Gorgias means 'speech is to the mind as drugs are to the body', which gives him opportunities for antithesis and chiasmus (δύναμις...τάξιν...τάξις...φύσιν). Isocrates 8.39 makes a similar comparison, perhaps copying it from Gorgias: τῶν μὲν περὶ τὸ σῶμα νοσημάτων πολλαὶ θεραπεῖαι καὶ παντοδαπαὶ τοῖς ἰατροῖς εὕρηνται, ταῖς δὲ ψυχαῖς ταῖς ἀγνοούσαις καὶ γεμούσαις πονηρῶν ἐπιθυμιῶν οὐδέν ἐστιν ἄλλο φάρμακον πλὴν λόγος, 'for bodily diseases many cures of various kinds have been discovered by doctors, but for minds which are ignorant and full of base desires there is no remedy but speech'. Plato *Gorgias* 464b (and elsewhere) adapts the comparison to his own views.

τάξιν...τάξις: the arrangement of the mind is its disposition or character; the arrangement of medicines is the prescription of them. (LSJ ought to cite this passage under τάξις II.3.b, not under VI, where *'Pal.'* is an error for *'Hel.'*.)

ἄλλα χυμὸς: a good medieval emendation of ἀλλαχοῦ. The meaning of χυμοί is 'humours', fluids in the body causing illness or health.

ἐξεφαρμάκευσαν καὶ ἐγοήτευσαν: these striking metaphors recall the references to sorcery in 10 as well as to drugs in 14, and so round off the whole discussion of speech in 8-14.

15 τὴν τετάρτην αἰτίαν: the four possible causes of Helen's elopement were listed in 6.

τῷ τετάρτῳ λόγῳ: 'the fourth section of my speech' (LSJ λόγος VI.3.d).

ἃ γὰρ ὁρῶμεν: love is an emotion caused by someone who is seen. Gorgias therefore proceeds to discuss the powerful effect which things seen have on people's behaviour, and gives various kinds of sight as examples. We are not responsible for the nature of what we see; so, he argues, we are not responsible for the effects which those sights have on our characters.

ἕκαστον: Bekker's emendation of ἕκαστος.

τυποῦται: the same metaphor as in 13.

16 One type of sight which affects people's behaviour is a sight which is frightening. Terror and shock may be caused either by a sight which foreshadows frightful events in the future (16), or by the sight of frightful events happening in the present (17 ἤδη...νόημα), or by recollection in the mind's eye of frightful events seen in the past (17 πολλοὶ...φρονήματι).

The textual problems in 16 have been discussed in detail by F. Donadi

(*Bollettino dell'Istituto di Filologia Greca, Padova* 4 [1977-8] 48-77). He rightly rejects a number of conjectures by various editors, but I do not find his own restoration of the text satisfactory. His principal suggestion is that the passage refers not to the sight of a real army, but to the representation of one in a tragedy; he postulates a revival of *Seven Against Thebes* in or about the year 405, and believes that to be the date of the *Encomium of Helen*. But in fact there is nothing in Gorgias' text to show that he is referring to a stage performance, and in particular the words φεύγουσιν ἐκπλαγέντες suit neither a chorus nor an audience.

ἐπὶ πολεμίᾳ ὁπλίσει: the reading is doubtful. The manuscripts' readings are ἐπὶ πολεμίοις ὁπλίσει (A) and ἐπὶ πολεμι' ὁπλίσει (X), to which ὁπλίσῃ is added, probably as a conjecture. With A's reading the point of ὁπλίσει is obscure. Most editors adopt ὁπλίσῃ, as a verb to be taken with ὅταν, but there is no subject for it. I have therefore adopted Sauppe's conjecture πολεμίᾳ, which enables ὁπλίσει to be taken with ἐπί.

τοῦ μὲν ἀλεξητήριον: swords and spearheads were made of iron, shields of bronze. We must take ἀλεξητήριον, which is an adjective qualifying κόσμον, as 'offensive', though I know of no other passage where it is used to make a contrast with defensive armour. For the chiastic arrangement of χαλκοῦ...προβλήματα, cf. 3 τοῦ μὲν γενομένου...Διός.

προβλήματα: 'shields'; cf. Aiskhylos *Seven Against Thebes* 539-40 ἐν χαλκηλάτῳ σάκει, κυκλωτῷ σώματος προβλήματι, 'on a bronze shield, the rounded covering of his body'. Since this, unlike ἀλεξητήριον, is a noun, there is no reason to reject the plural as several editors do.

ἐπιθεάσηται: another doubtful reading. The manuscripts give εἰ θεάσεται, but the future tense has no point here. Sauppe conjectured the aorist subjunctive θεάσηται to go with ὅταν. To keep closer to the manuscripts I have conjectured ἐπιθεάσηται.

ἡ ὄψις: subject both of ἐπιθεάσηται and ἐταράχθη. 'The sight is alarmed' seems to refer to the reaction of the eyes; in colloquial English a person's eyes 'pop out of his head'. Gorgias regards this as a cause, not a result, of the alarm of the mind.

<ὡς>: a good conjecture by Diels. The attempt of Donadi (op. cit. 71) to defend κινδύνου τοῦ μέλλοντος ὄντος as meaning 'in the presence of a danger proceeding from the future' is unconvincing because it gives an impossible sense to the dependent genitive.

φεύγουσιν: the subject is a vague unexpressed 'people'. Possibly πολλοὶ has been lost from the text by haplography before πολλάκις.

ἀμέλεια is my emendation of ἀλήθεια: cf. *CQ* 11 (1961) 121. The law requires a soldier to fight, not to run away.

εἰσφκίσθη: 'is implanted'; cf. Plato *Republic* 424d ἡ γοῦν παρανομία...κατὰ

38

σμικρὸν εἰσοικισαμένη ἠρέμα ὑπορρεῖ πρὸς τὰ ἤθη τε καὶ τὰ ἐπιτηδεύματα, 'lawlessness, gradually implanting itself, creeps into conduct and behaviour'.

ἀμελῆσαι: an emendation of ἀσμενίσαι, first proposed in the sixteenth century by Canter, as Donadi (op. cit. 58) points out. Donadi himself defends ἀσμενίσαι, taking it to refer to the pleasure of the audience in watching a tragedy and undergoing a κάθαρσις of fear; but Gorgias is not Aristotle, and there is no reference to tragedy in this passage.

κρινομένου: 'awarded' (LSJ κρίνω II.3.a). τοῦ καλοῦ is the honour or high reputation which soldiers gain if they do their duty, whereas τοῦ ἀγαθοῦ is material advantage.

17 ματαίοις πόνοις: worry for which there is no real justification. The whole sentence refers to ill effects continuing after a frightening sight is already past.

τῷ φρονήματι: here indistinguishable from τῇ ψυχῇ.

τὰ μὲν... is balanced not by δέ but by ἀλλὰ μὴν... in the next sentence, to mean 'So much for...; but there is also...'.

παραλείπεται: 'are passed over', because it is unnecessary to give further examples of the effects of frightening sights.

18 The next example is the powerful effect of the sight of beautiful paintings and sculpture.

σωμάτων: 'elements', 'individual items', expanses of paint of various shapes and sizes.

νόσον: Dobree's emendation of ὅσον. There is something 'wrong' with one's eyes, because one seems to see a man when one is really looking at paint or stone.

τέρπειν: my emendation of ποθεῖν. Presumably some scribe's eye slipped to πόθον in the next line. An antonym of λυπεῖν is clearly required, and τέρπειν is the most obvious one (cf. 14 and the first sentence of 18), but others are possible; Diels conjectured κηλεῖν.

19 προθυμίαν καὶ ἄμιλλαν ἔρωτος: 'an amatory eagerness and competition'. The use of ἄμιλλα for a mental or emotional attitude is unusual; I have found no exact parallel (unless the conjecture ἀμίλλη is accepted in Herodas 6.68), but cf. Sophokles *Elektra* 494 γάμων ἀμιλλήμαθ', 'eagerness for marriage'.

ὅς refers to ἔρωτος. After εἰ the verb ἐστι is understood, as at the beginning of 8.

ἔχων is my emendation of the manuscripts' θεῶν: cf. *CQ* 11 (1961) 121-2.

ὁ ἥσσων: masculine; not just Helen, therefore, but any man or woman, being weaker than love.

νόσημα...: note the series of rhyming nouns in -ημα in this sentence, with further rhymes in - τέον, - ης, - εύμασι, and - αις.

ἦλθε γάρ, ὡς ἦλθε: 'for it comes, when it does come', yet another aorist for a regular occurrence. The point of ὡς ἦλθε is similar to that of 16 ἐλθοῦσα. Not 'she came <to Troy>', because ὁ ἥσσων turned the subject from the individual Helen to any human being in love; the particular case of Helen is not reintroduced until her name is mentioned in the first sentence of 20.

ψυχῆς ἀγρεύμασιν: 'snares for the mind', objective genitive, as in Aiskhylos *Libation-bearers* 998 ἄγρευμα θηρός.

γνώμης βουλεύμασι: 'intentions of the mind'. Here γνώμη means virtually the same as ψυχή, but this genitive is subjective. Thus ψυχῆς and γνώμης sound parallel but their syntactical function is actually different, just as with ψυχῆς and δόξης in 10; cf. note on 2 τῶν συμφορῶν μνήμη.

ἔρωτος: reflexive in sense, since ἔρως is the subject of the sentence. Love comes by love's own force, not by carefully contrived arrangements.

20 εἴτε...: the four possible explanations of Helen's conduct, listed in 6 and discussed in turn in 6-19, are now in retrospect listed in reverse order.

<ὄψει>: conjectured by Immisch. It is clearly needed in order to make the phrase parallel to εἴτε λόγῳ πεισθεῖσα, etc.

πάντως: not just 'completely', but 'in all four cases'.

21 τῇ γνώμῃ ἦν: my emendation of the unsatisfactory readings of the manuscripts (τῷ μώμῳ ὂν ἔν A, τῷ νόμῳ ὂν X); cf. *CQ* 11 (1961) 117.

παίγνιον: one may imagine the twinkle in Gorgias' eyes as he reveals in the very last word that he regards the whole parodoxical composition as a game.

www.ingramcontent.com/pod-product-compliance
Ingram Content Group UK Ltd.
Pitfield, Milton Keynes, MK11 3LW, UK
UKHW020737280225
455688UK00012B/715